WILD ANIMALS
of the AMERICAN ROCKIES

~ *by* ~
Kevin Van Tighem

The Blackfeet say that Napi came here after he created the animals and taught people how to live. He came at last to a place where gray cliffs rear high into the sky and newborn waters cascade from summer snows. In that place, there are bear tracks in the mud. Elk bugle. Wild animals exhale the breath of their creator. It is like that there, even now.

WILD ANIMALS
of the AMERICAN ROCKIES

Altitude Publishing Ltd.
#309-4255 South Buckley Road, Aurora, CO 80013

Cataloguing in Publication Data
Van Tighem, Kevin, 1952–
Wild animals of the American Rockies

ISBN 1-55265-013-8

1. Mammals--Rocky Mountains. 2. Mammals--Rocky Mountains--
Pictorial works I. Title.
QL719.R63V36 1999   599'.0978   C99-910187-0

Printed and bound in Canada
by Friesen Printers

Production

Design & art direction	Stephen Hutchings
Editor	Sabrina Grobler
Financial management	Laurie Smith

Altitude GreenTree Program
Altitude Publishing will plant twice as many trees
as were used in the manufacturing of this product.

CONTENTS

WILD ANIMALS

The San Juans, Sangre de Cristos and Medicine Bow Mountains. The Wind River Range and the Absarokas. The Grand Tetons. Going-to-the-Sun. Kananaskis. Mount Assiniboine. The Columbia Icefield.

The names of these high places resonate. The high backbone of the North American continent stretches from Mexico to Yukon, through seven states, two Canadian provinces, one territory and three nations. This is the Rocky Mountain West, where that which is most wild and free in the American imagination still lingers. Wind tears clouds apart against the stillness of these mountains; wild animals give birth, live, and die upon their slopes.

The Rocky Mountains have stood against the sky for more than 45 million years. Their stone is far older than that. The wild animals that dwell upon their slopes and among their folds are young by comparison, but their kinds have dwelt here far longer than we who travel up into those mountains to visit them.

The ranges stand apart—some like islands of up-turned stone, adrift upon the dry West's tawny plains; others connecting to adjacent ranges across narrow valleys or low passes. Snow patches linger on the summits late into summer. Some never melt. In Glacier National Park and the Canadian Rockies, the blue ice of glaciers underlies the perennial snows in some high basins. Steep-walled cirques and U-shaped valleys in Rocky Mountains National Park reveal the tracks of similar glaciers now long-gone from the southern Rockies.

Limestone, sandstone, granite and quartzite—carved by ice and water, worn by wind, worked by millennia of freezing and thawing—give each range its distinctive character, and each peak its shape. Weathered rock, worked by the roots of alpine plants and mountain forests, spreads a thin veneer of soil over the bones of the earth. An intricate mosaic of vegetation springs from mountain soils—grassy on the southern slopes where sun and wind wick moisture away, dark-forested on the north sides of mountains, shredded vertically by snow avalanches, and patterned by the distribution of water across the complex folds and twists of the Rocky Mountain landscape.

Rocky Mountain wildlife lives in three dimensions. Their habitats are patchy and diverse. Summer is brief and cool in the high country. Winter brings deep snow, prolonged cold, treacherous travel and, to the unlucky, starvation.

Some, like marmots and black bears, feed and give birth during the green wealth of an alpine summer, then wait out the winter's scarcity by sleeping in underground dens. Others, like red squirrels and pikas, lay in winter supplies of food and take advantage of the insulating snow cover to escape the cold of winter. Still others, like elk and mule deer, migrate out of the high country to wind-blown foothills and the edges of the low-elevation plains where snow stays shallow in winter.

Humans, too, are most abundant in the Rocky Mountain West during summer. We journey from afar to visit the great national parks—Rocky Mountain, Yellowstone, Glacier, Banff, Jasper—and to restore our spirits with the peace and splendor of some of earth's most inspiring landscapes. Our roads snake up the valleys that separate the mountain ranges; our destinations are high basins and ridge-top trails that take us close to heaven. Sometimes we wish we could remain forever.

Wild animals do. They were here long before our roads and cities. If we study to understand them and strive to show their mountain landscapes the respect they deserve, they will be here long after us. This is their home. In learning how the elk, bobcat, pack rat, mountain lion and bighorn sheep find food, protection and freedom amid their secret places of stone and stillness, we can make it our home too.

BEARS

Humans and bears have shared the mountains for millennia. We have a lot in common—from our flatfooted tracks to our omnivorous diets and low birth rates.

Native Americans have long considered the bear an older brother. Bears taught aboriginal people which plants are good to eat or to use as medicines. In the legends of many tribes, the bear is a sacred animal that brought food to the people and showed them how to live.

Few people now experience the intimacy with animals that North America's aboriginal people once enjoyed. Like the early native people of the Rockies, modern Americans fear wild bears. We no longer, however, respect them as older brothers.

In the brave light of day we watch bears from safety, as strangers seeking entertainment, thrilled by our fears. Both bear and human suffer from such estrangement. Humans lose because our fear and the shallowness of our understanding isolate us farther from the wild, living world that is our true home. Bears lose because our fear and disrespect make them dangerous, and we kill them.

The Rocky Mountain West remains a place of hope. Here, perhaps, we can relearn the humility and respect that will make us, again, brother and sister to the bear.

Top: Bears range widely, foraging on roots, insects, newborn ungulates, grasses, berries, nuts and other foods.

Opposite: From April through early November, a black bear's sensitive nose leads it from one food source to another.

Top: Less than a year old, black bear cubs taste dandelions in a mountain meadow.

Opposite: Ears focussed on whatever surprised it, a black bear stands for a better look, deciding whether to flee, fight, or resume foraging for food.

BLACK BEARS

Unlike the endangered grizzly bear, black bears remain common throughout the Rocky Mountain West. Their favourite habitats overlap with ours—forested valley bottoms and stream sides. Black bears eat dandelions, horsetails and other plants that thrive on roadsides and other human-made habitats.

For thousands of years, black bears found rich pickings around the edges of camps and settlements. Some Native American tribes placed their dead on platforms in trees to protect them from scavenging bears. Their dogs cleaned up camp scraps. Native people had no choice but to prevent black bears from raiding their camps for food: the price of failure might be starvation or an attack by a hungry bear grown bold.

Modern visitors to black bear country face a similar challenge. Today, however, most humans travel in motor vehicles, sleep behind walls, and need rarely cope with the consequences of our failures. Our efforts to keep black bears from becoming addicted to human food or garbage have less to do with our safety than with concern for the well-being of animals we respect.

Top: There is no more dangerous wild animal in the Rockies than a female grizzly determined to protect her young.

Opposite: Black bears depend on enlightened behavior from humans to keep them out of danger. A fed bear, many park rangers say, is a dead bear.

GRIZZLY BEARS

Old Ephraim once roamed the high country from northern Mexico north to Alaska. Today the grizzly is endangered in the U.S. Rockies. A few hundred survive in the greater Yellowstone ecosystem and parts of northern Montana and Idaho, but most of the West's surviving grizzly bears live in the mountains of British Columbia, Alberta, Yukon and Alaska.

The grizzly's reputation for fierceness is overblown. Montana and Alberta ranchers live in relative peace with the great bears. Thousands of hikers share the high country with grizzlies every summer in Glacier, Banff and Jasper National Parks. Some day, when we are ready, we may welcome the grizzly back to their ancestral homes in Colorado, New Mexico and other western states. Many people feel that bringing the grizzly home would right a historical wrong and restore the wild to the waiting Rockies.

UNGULATES

What strange extravagance of nature decreed that hoofed animals should carry great weights around on their heads? A bighorn ram's horns or a bull moose's antlers may weigh more than 40 pounds. Ungulates must survive bitterly cold winters and deep snow. Heavy horns or antlers waste precious energy.

Only the males of most species can spare the energy needed to grow large antlers and horns. Females put all their energy into the precious fetuses growing in their bodies. Unlike males, they must accumulate body fat to nurture offspring.

The massive horns of a bighorn ram or the spreading antlers of a bull elk or mule deer buck are proof of superiority. Only animals with sufficient skill and strength to survive several years acquire such status symbols. Large horns or antlers prove that these males are healthy, of superior genetic stock, and likely to pass on their vigor to their offspring.

Ungulates mate in the fall. The males with the most impressive headgear do most of the breeding. Then, as winter snows accumulate and food becomes hard to find, the females and young gather on the best winter ranges. Exhausted males, their work done, retire to less friendly terrain. If they die of their own too-much or fall victim to predators, it matters little to the population. Next spring, a new generation will carry on their legacy.

Top: White-tailed deer frequent the aspen parkland and river-bottom forests of the larger valleys.

Opposite: Thousands of years of natural selection by wolves, cougars and humans have made the white-tailed deer exceptionally alert and fleet of foot.

Top: A rutting mule deer buck has a swollen neck and a steady, purposeful walk as he searches the November woods for does.

Right: A doe mule deer and her fawn listen in all directions for potential danger.

Opposite: A truly western deer, the mule deer is larger than the whitetail and frequents more open country.

Top: Elk, like other deer, grow new antlers each year. Large-antlered bulls —the most genetically superior, well-fed and prime-aged males—dominate smaller bulls.

Right: Cow elk and newborn calves gather into herds. More eyes and ears offer greater safety from predators.

Opposite: Each September, rutting bull elk fill the frosty mornings with frenzied bugling as they gather harems of cows and compete for breeding rights.

Top: A bull elk's velvet-covered antlers grow so fast that they become hot to the touch.

Right: A nursing cow elk still wears last winter's shaggy hair. Other elk shed earlier.

Left: Elk eat leaves and buds in summer, along with grasses and other green plants.

Top: A moose immerses its whole head to eat submerged pondweeds. This bull's growing antlers are covered with velvet.

Right: Cow moose: listening, smelling and watching for danger.

Opposite: A young bull moose displays its ponderous nose, palmate antlers, long legs and the characteristic—but seemingly useless—"bell" on its neck.

Top: Deep grooves mark each year's growth of a bighorn ram's horn. This full-curl ram is at least eight years old.

Left: Bighorns winter where wind or mild weather keep the snow shallow.

Opposite: A mature ram's swollen neck and enlarged scrotum are signs of the November breeding season.

Top: Small-horned, younger rams give way to dominant, large-horned rams. They rarely enjoy much success in breeding.

Left: Within a few hours of birth, bighorn lambs can run, climb and clamber around on cliffs where they are safe from predators.

Top: In late fall, bighorn rams like this massive old-timer will cross broad valleys to travel from one concentration of ewes to another.

Left: Dominance battles result when rams of similar size compete for status. To gain power, both rams rise high on their hind legs.

Right: Upon contact, bodies telescope and necks curl under. Spongy bones at the base of the horns protect their brains.

Top: Spongy hoof pads, a low center of gravity and an incredible ability to balance and turn enable mountain goats to perform astonishing climbing feats.

Right: Two layers of dense white wool protect mountain goats from wind and cold.

Opposite: Slow, methodical, incredibly tough: mountain goats thrive on the toughest terrain the Rockies have to offer.

Top: Herds of plains bison once wintered in the windblown grasslands along the flanks of the Rocky Mountains. Their grazing helped shape the native prairie.

Left: A lone bull bison. Only a few captive herds remain of the more than 60 million bison that once ranged the West.

Top: Pronghorns rely on sharp eyes and incredible speed to avoid predators on the open plains.

Right: A newborn pronghorn lies first, waiting for its mother to return from her feeding.

CATS

Cats hunt alone by night, prowling the shadows and watching for prey. A cat's eyes are specialized for night work, equipped with cells that double how much light they see. Focusing on the slightest movement, a hunting cat freezes, crouches low, and fixes its prey with an uncanny stare.

Only three kinds of wild cat prowl the Rocky Mountain West. The endangered lynx is least common, limited to the old growth forests and deep snow country of the northern Rockies. Large, snowshoe-like feet enable lynxes to hunt their favourite prey—the snowshoe hare—in deep snow. Bobcats are less rare, especially in mountain canyons in the southern Rockies where cottontail rabbits abound. Unlike their northern cousins, bobcats prefer low elevations where winter snow remains shallow.

The mountain lion is the most abundant and widespread wild cat in the Rockies. Mountain lions stalk deer the way house cats stalk mice. One paw at a time, body low, eyes and ears fixed on its prey, the tawny shadow eases to within a few feet, then races from hiding. If luck is on its side, the lion will grasp its prey around the shoulders with sharp-clawed forefeet and bite through the neck and throat. Most often, however, the mountain lion's quarry escapes unharmed.

Mountain lions are the most efficient deer predators in the Rockies, outperforming the wolf where both share the same habitat.

Top: A female mountain lion—also commonly called a cougar—with her young kitten.

Opposite: Mountain lions—shy and elusive hunters that rarely bother humans—range from Mexico to northern British Columbia.

Top: Long legs and oversized feet enable the Canada lynx to hunt its favorite prey—the snowshoe hare—in deep winter snows.

Left: The rarely seen bobcat is common in some parts of the Rockies. Their small feet force them to avoid deep snow.

Opposite: Sensitive whiskers on their faces and the bottoms of their feet help wild cats feel their way through darkened forests.

DOGS

Late evening: the mountains are silhouetted against the fading sky. A coyote yelps. Another replies; then a hysterical cacophony of barks and shrieks shatters the evening calm. Far off—beginning on a low note, rising gradually, then breaking away to a trailing moan—a more fearsome voice issues from the shadows. The silence after the wolf howl is brittle with expectancy. Every animal in the valley, no doubt, has paused for a moment to test the breeze and listen. The coyotes remain discreetly silent. Something will die tonight.

Of all predators, the wild dogs arouse the strongest human emotions. Sociable, intelligent predators, wolves and coyotes have survived a century of persecution.

Eradicated in the 1950s, wolves recolonized northern Montana on their own from Canada; recently, biologists have started new wild populations in Wyoming, Idaho and New Mexico. The smaller red fox is no doubt as glad of the wolf's return as are the raven, magpie, chickadee and skunk. All scavenge meals from the remains of wolf kills.

Wolf packs hunt animals as big as moose. Killing such large prey demands teamwork, and provides more than enough food for pack members to share. Foxes hunt alone. Their small prey requires no teamwork and provides no leftovers.

The adaptable coyote can assume either lifestyle, hunting rodents solo or teaming up for big game.

Top: Sharp-nosed, big-eared and intelligent, the coyote usually hunts mice and small animals. Packs of coyotes, however, can kill deer or even small elk.

Opposite: A timber wolf howls to communicate with other pack members. Less common than the coyote, wolves are recolonizing the Rocky Mountain West.

Top: Wolves are built for travel. Packs range widely across the landscape, hunting deer, elk and other large prey.

Left: Coyotes can hear mice beneath the snow, even at distances.

Top: Coyote pups rarely venture far from the safety of the den.

Right: Curious, cautious and clever, coyotes have survived—and thrived—despite a century of persecution.

Top: Fox kits, like other young dogs, chew at the lips of returning parents. The chewing triggers a gag reflex, and the adult regurgitates a partly digested meal for the hungry kit.

Right: The fox relies on acute hearing and a finely tuned nose to find mice and other small prey.

Opposite: Swift foxes live on the dry plains where they hunt prairie dogs, jackrabbits and small rodents.

SMALL MAMMALS

F ur trappers penetrated the Rocky Mountain West in the 1700s. They soon came to hate the wolverine. Wolverines, however, welcomed this new kind of human. Wolverines travel widely and scavenge aggressively, especially in winter, to find enough food. Trappers made life easier by setting traps along mountain valleys for beaver, marten, mink and other creatures. Wolverines quickly learned to rob traplines and raid trappers' cabins.

Trapping's time is mostly past in the Rockies. Many furbearers are endangered now from logging and habitat loss, not from cold steel. Wolverines—where they survive in the northern Rockies—have had to revert to old ways of finding food. One of those old ways is to hunt porcu-

pines in the snowy timberline country of the Waterton-Glacier International Peace Park, Banff and other Canadian national parks. A wolverine will willingly risk a face full of quills if there is a chance of fat-rich meal of porcupine meat.

Porcupines remain active in winter because their preferred food—tree sap-wood—is always available. Beavers, which also eat tree bark, build underwater caches of twigs and freshly cut branches so they can continue to eat after their ponds freeze. Marmots, whose summer meadows produce a brief abundance of greenery, simply curl up in their dens and sleep the hungry winter away.

Top: A beaver recycles an aspen tree into food and construction materials.

Opposite: Beavers cut down aspens to build dams and to eat the bark and twigs. After a year or two, their aspen supply exhausted, the large rodents die or move on. The aspen re-sprout from their roots; eventually beavers return.

Top: Raccoons are rare in the Rockies, confined mostly to river bottoms and canyons at low elevations.

Left: Foraging near water, raccoons leave distinctive hand-like tracks in mud.

Top: Porcupines are common in some timberline areas, and at lower elevations in deciduous forests and shrubbery. They feed on bark and twigs.

Right: Dense guard hairs conceal a forest of barbed quills which protect the porcupine when predators threaten.

Top: The wolverine, rare but still widespread in the Canadian Rockies, is an endangered species in the mountains of Montana and Idaho. This determined hunter and scavenger is the largest member of the weasel family.

Left: Badgers are built for digging. Long claws and powerful leg muscles enable them to dig up burrowing rodents.

Top: Old-growth forests in Canada's mountain national parks protect the American marten, but this tree-climbing weasel is endangered in the northern U.S. Rockies.

Bottom left: Unlike its larger relatives the long-tailed weasel turns white in winter. It hunts small rodents.

Bottom right: Long-tailed weasel in summer pelage.

SMALLEST MAMMALS

A deer mouse may give birth three or more times a year. A single pair of deer mice could theoretically multiply to more than 600 within 12 months.

Small mammals like deer mice live short lives and breed prolifically. They are abundant, too; many more small mammals can occupy the same space as only a few larger mammals. A grizzly bear, for example, may have a home range of more than 1,200 square miles. Within that bear's home range, there are millions of mice, squirrels, chipmunks and ground squirrels.

It is fortunate, and no coincidence, that small mammals are so abundant. Grizzly bears need not worry about being eaten. Smaller mammals, on the other hand, provide meals for hawks, eagles, prairie falcons, owls, martens, badgers, weasels, coyotes, foxes, lynx and many other animals.

Mountain winters are hard. Small mammals must fatten and reproduce during the short period between April and October when vegetation is most lush. Some, like pikas and woodrats, store dried vegetation during the summer so they can eat during the long winter. Others, like chipmunks and ground squirrels, hibernate in underground dens all winter. Mice and voles hide beneath the insulating snow cover. Only the red squirrel remains active above the snow to greet winter visitors to the Rockies.

Top: Oversized ears, like organic radiators, keep jackrabbits cool when the summer sun bakes the Rockies' grassy flanks.

Opposite: Marmots burrow beneath boulders to avoid predators. After fattening all summer, they sleep the winter away underground.

Top: Numerous chipmunk species thrive among the forests and shrub thickets of the Rockies.

Left: Deer mice are the most abundant of several species of mice and voles that serve as prey for coyotes, martens, weasels, hawks, owls and other predators.

Top: Commonly misidentified as a chipmunk, the golden-mantled ground squirrel has a distinctive eye ring and buff-colored shoulders.

Right: Pikas are tiny rabbits that scurry about gathering and drying grass all summer long. Pikas store their hay in boulder piles. Beneath the snow-pack, they feed on it all winter long.

Top: Richardson's ground squirrel thrives in shortgrass prairie along the flanks of the Rockies.

Left: The red squirrel is the most widespread tree-dwelling squirrel in the Rocky Mountain West. Common and noisy, it is fiercely territorial.

Top: Meadow voles search through the underbrush for food.

Bottom right: The most strikingly marked of the squirrels, 13-lined ground squirrels favor bunchgrass prairie along the eastern flanks of the Rockies.

Bottom left: All ground squirrels hibernate. This one is gathering nesting material for its underground winter den.

Top: Although it lives underground, the rock squirrel spends considerable time perching on rock outcrops or trees where it keeps an eye out for danger.

Left: Abert's squirrel thrives in forests of ponderosa pine and Gambel oak.

Right: Cottontail rabbits breed prolifically—a good thing since bobcats, foxes and other predators rely on them as food.

THE AUTHOR

Through his writings, Kevin Van Tighem communicates his passion for the creatures that inhabit the alpine wilderness. Having worked in Banff, Jasper, Yoho, Elk Island, Waterton Lakes, Glacier and Mt. Revelstoke national parks for the Canadian Parks Service and the Canadian Wildlife Service, he has come to know and love the wildlife of the Rocky

Mountains. In his numerous magazine articles and his book, *Wild Animals of Western Canada*, he describes the beauty and integrity of the animals with a sense of awe and wonder.

Author's Note: While most of the photographic images in this book are of wild animals living free, some difficult-to-find species or behaviors were photographed under captive conditions.

PHOTOGRAPHY CREDITS

All photos in this book were taken by **Dennis and Esther Schmidt**, with the exception of the following:

Lu Carbyn: 41
Jim Osterberg: 54 (a & b)
Brian Wolitski: 47 (b & c), 53 (a)